THE
FUNNYBONE BOOK
OF JOKES AND RIDDLES

Q. Why should you read this book?
A. To bone up on laughter!

A Platt & Munk ALL ABOARD BOOK™

THE FUNNYBONE BOOK
OF JOKES AND RIDDLES

By Carol Thompson

Illustrated by Vincent Andriani

Platt & Munk, Publishers

Copyright © 1987 by Platt & Munk, Publishers, a division of Grosset & Dunlap. Illustrations copyright © 1987 by Vincent Andriani. All rights reserved. Grosset & Dunlap is a member of The Putnam Publishing Group, New York. ALL ABOARD BOOKS is a trademark of The Putnam Publishing Group. Published simultaneously in Canada. Printed in the U.S.A. Library of Congress Catalog Card Number: 86-81157 ISBN 0-448-19080-X
B C D E F G H I J

SPORTS SILLIES

Q. Why didn't the golfer wear shoes?
A. Because he had a hole in one.

Q. How do you congratulate a champion octopus?

A. You shake his hand, hand, hand, hand, hand, hand. hand, hand,

THE WINNER

Q. Why did Tarzan lose the tennis match?
A. Because he played against a cheetah.

Q. How many sides does a bowling ball have?
A. Just two. Inside and outside.

LUNCHROOM LAUGHS

Polly: Why are you eating nickels?
Esther: Because the teacher wants to see some change in me.

Q. What table has no legs?   A. The multiplication table.

Seymour: What kind of bread is that?
Anita: Hole wheat, of course.

Q. What has lots of teeth but never eats?
A. A comb!

FUNNYBONE CRACKS

Q. Why did the skeleton get such a high score on the quiz?
A. Because he got the bone-us question.

Q. What do you get when you cross a tramp with a skeleton?
A. A ho-bone.

Q. Why didn't the skeleton use a towel after his bath?
A. Because he was already bone dry.

Q. If you cross a famous detective with a skeleton, what do you get?
A. Sherlock Bones.

LITTLE STINKERS

Q. Are skunks stupid?
A. Well, they don't have good scents.

Q. Why did the skunk spray the courtroom?
A. Because the judge said, "Odor in the court!"

Q. How does Ms. Skunk pay her bills?
A. With dollars and scents.

Q. What did the little skunk say about the ice cream?
A. "It'smelted!"

GROCERY GIGGLES

Q. What has eyes and goes spudt-spudt?
A. An outboard potato.

LOBSTERS

Q. Why did the cookie cry?
A. Because his mommy was a wa-fer so long.

COOL JOKES

Bob Sled: Why can't a
car get cold?
Iggy Lou: Because it
has a muffler!

Q. What falls down and
doesn't get hurt?
A. Snow.

Q. Where do polar bears vote?
A. The North Polls.

Q. What do penguins ride?
A. Ice-cycles.

MORE LITTLE STINKERS

Q. What is the most famous skunk statue in Egypt?
A. The Stinx.

Q. How long did it take to build?
A. A scentury.

Q. Why was the little skunk
   sitting on the swing?

A. Because his mom scent
   him out to play.

Q. Are baby skunks cute?
A. Yes, they're odorable!

WHAT A SCARY FAIR!

Q. What is a spook's favorite carnival ride?
A. The roller ghoster.

Q. Where did the vampire learn to read?
A. Ghoul school.

Q. What is a monster's favorite snack?
A. An "I-scream" sandwich.

Q. What is a ghost's favorite kind of pie?
A. Boo-berry.

ELEPHANT TRICKS

Q. What do you get when you cross peanuts with an elephant?
A. Peanut butter that never forgets, or ...

A. an elephant that sticks to the roof of your mouth.

Q. What do you feed a blue elephant for breakfast?
A. Blue Elephant Toasties.

Q. What do you feed a pink elephant for breakfast?
A. You tell the pink elephant not to breathe
   until he turns blue. Then you feed him
   Blue Elephant Toasties.

COOKIE CUT-UPS

Q. Why did the Gingerbread Boy stay home from school?
A. Because he felt crumby.

Q. What did the Gingerbread Boy find under his blanket?
A. A cookie sheet.

TOWN TICKLERS

Q. Why is the library the tallest building in town?
A. Because it has the most stories.

Q. What goes from one town to the next without moving?
A. Railroad tracks.

Q. What's long and thin and says, "Hith, hith?"
A. A cobra with a lisp.

Q. Why did the ostrich hide his head in a hole?
A. Because a bird in the sand is worth two in the bush.

JESTS IN THE WEST

Q. What does a cowboy like on his pancakes?
A. Maple stirrup.

Q. What's the best way to catch a wild stallion?
A. Have someone throw it to you.

Q. What famous cowboy wears a mask?
A. The Bone Stranger.

SLEEPY SLAPSTICK

Q. What question can you never answer with a "yes"?
A. "Are you asleep?"